A Woman's Guide to

Discipling

Inspiration, Advice, and Practical Tools for Helping Others Grow

A Woman's Guide to

Discipling

DANA YEAKLEY

NAVPRESS

Discipleship Inside Out™

Discipleship Inside Out™

NavPress is the publishing ministry of The Navigators, an international Christian organization and leader in personal spiritual development. NavPress is committed to helping people grow spiritually and enjoy lives of meaning and hope through personal and group resources that are biblically rooted, culturally relevant, and highly practical.

For a free catalog go to www.NavPress.com
or call 1.800.366.7788 in the United States or 1.800.839.4769 in Canada.

ISBN-13: 978-1-60006-714-3

Cover design by Arvid Wallen
Cover image by Shutterstock

Some of the anecdotal illustrations in this book are true to life and are included with the permission of the persons involved. All other illustrations are composites of real situations, and any resemblance to people living or dead is coincidental.

Printed in the United States of America

1 2 3 4 5 6 7 8 / 14 13 12 11 10

Contents

Acknowledgments

THE CONTENT OF this workbook has been handed down from generation to generation of women. It is truly written by women for women. Because of that, I have many people to recognize and thank.

Much of the content in this workbook first came to me many years ago in the form of personal training and mentoring given to me by Deb and Lee Maschhoff.

In 2000, with the help of my administrative assistant, Ellen Susman, I compiled a workbook called *The Gentle Art of Discipling Women* for the collegiate staff of The Navigators. In it I gathered what I had learned from the Maschhoffs and my own experiences discipling women. Thank you, Ellen, for your vital help in bringing the original workbook into being.

As the positive responses to the original workbook multiplied, NavPress encouraged me to adapt and expand the content for a broader audience than just Navigator staff members. That is what you hold in your hands. In expanding the content, I drew on the hearts and experiences of many other women who disciple women: Cathy Bowman, Lori Butler, Ann Chris, Stacy Frazer, Sherry Graf, Heather Hanneman, Meaghan Hart, Kim Havenstein, Jennifer Johnson, Sue Kline, Beth Luebe, Deb Maschhoff, Gretchen Riedel, Melanie Rogers, Carol Rugg, and Ellen Susman. These women's lives demonstrate what we are aiming for in this workbook.

Props to Sue Kline, editor and lover of God and people, who helped me put into words what I really mean.

And finally, I want to thank my husband, Tom, who continues to encourage me to be all God has made me to be.

Introduction

MANY YEARS AGO, my husband, Tom, and I met a couple who lived with joy and purpose. We loved being around them and joined a group that met at their home. This group studied the Bible to discover how to live a life that was pleasing to God.

After some time in the group, Tom and I asked this couple if they would meet with us individually to help us grow in our walk with God and in our marriage. Later they told us they had been praying we would ask them to do just that!

I began meeting with Deb, the wife, and Tom began meeting with Lee, her husband. Sometimes the four of us would get together to play cards, go out for dinner, or study the Bible. No matter what we did, we enjoyed being with them. We took in much from observing their lives, listening to what they shared from the Word, and trusting God together in prayer.

That was thirty-five years ago. Looking back, nothing has been as rewarding and life-changing as those years when this couple helped us grow spiritually. Because of their faithful friendship and godly example, we too began spending time with couples younger than ourselves to help them grow in knowing God and living for Him. We were not perfect by any means, but it was a joy to share our lives, the Word, and prayer with others.

I want others—you!—to know the joy of helping other women grow in their walk with Christ. That's why I compiled this guide. I say "compiled" because most of the content did not originate with me; it was received from women who have gone before me and next to me in helping other women grow. My goal is to launch, inspire, instruct, and give you skills for discipling others.

Chapters 1 through 3 are intended to be confidence builders. You will discover that "making disciples" (that is, helping others grow) is God's idea. His purposes and His heart permeate the last words of Christ to His disciples, words we call the Great Commission. And because God always equips us for what He asks us to do, you'll learn that you *can* make disciples, not because you are such a committed woman or even a capable woman but because God, through His Holy Spirit, will be with you and bring the growth in those you help.

Chapters 4 through 6 introduce you to some classic tools for helping other women grow spiritually. These tools come from The Navigators, an organization whose name is almost synonymous with discipleship. You will learn how to use these tools in the context of your own life, which will then prepare you to use them with those you disciple.

Chapters 7 through 9 will teach you skills that will help you disciple others. You will also receive the foundation you need to create your own collection of ideas and tools for helping other women grow in Christ.

Finally, in chapter 10, you will meet the Master Discipler, Jesus Christ, and receive insight and inspiration for your role as a discipler of women.

God is not looking for women who have it all together or are Bible experts. He is looking for women with available and tender hearts. He is looking for women who have a heart for Him and the faith to believe He can support them in whatever He calls them to do. Do you have a heart for God? Good, then read on!

The eyes of the LORD range throughout the earth to strengthen those whose hearts are fully committed to him. (2 Chronicles 16:9)

The Heart of a Discipler

MANY WOMEN I talk with feel inadequate or overwhelmed when they think about discipling other women. But in the face of those inadequacies, God has provided confidence builders.

In this workbook, we begin with a look into God's heart as revealed in Jesus' life and final words. Next we'll face our fears head-on and find the strength we have in Christ. Then we'll take inventory of our spiritual journeys thus far and discover what we have to offer others.

Chapter 1: Famous Last Words
Chapter 2: "Here Am I, Lord. Send Her!"
Chapter 3: The "B" Process

Famous Last Words

Go and make disciples.
(MATTHEW 28:19)

WHEN JESUS BEGAN His ministry—a ministry that lasted only three years—He didn't start a local church as we know churches. He did not take over a synagogue and start a revolution. He didn't preach in the arenas of the Roman Empire. Instead, Jesus invited twelve men to be with Him for three years, to go everywhere He went. And that is what happened. These "disciples," as they were called, observed His life: how He related to people, how He handled opposition and disappointment, what His priorities were. They listened as Jesus taught about God's kingdom and His ways. They noticed how Jesus showed His dependence on God the Father through prayer. In all these things, Jesus was modeling for His disciples exactly what He wanted them to become.

After His death, burial, and resurrection, Jesus appeared again to these disciples. He spent forty days with them, and then He spoke His last words to them before returning to His Father. I think we can all agree that last words are important. Jesus' last words were a command and contained His vision for reaching the world with the gospel. Not surprisingly, Jesus commanded His disciples to do what He had just spent three years doing: "Go, and as you are going, make disciples of all the nations!"

Let's look at Jesus' command as recorded by His disciple Matthew:

The eleven disciples went to Galilee, to the mountain where Jesus had told them to go. When they saw him, they worshiped him; but some doubted. Then Jesus came to them and said, "All authority in heaven and on earth has been given to me. Therefore *go and make disciples* of all nations, baptizing them in the name of the Father and of the Son and of the Holy Spirit, and teaching them to obey everything I have commanded you. And surely I am with you always, to the very end of the age." (Matthew 28:16-20, emphasis added)

1. Jesus' command is to "make disciples." How would you explain to another person what a disciple is?

2. Read John 8:30-32. Those following Jesus came to believe in Him. What did Jesus invite them to do that would prove that they were His disciples?

3. What does it mean to continue in His Word? Why is this so important?

4. Read Matthew 4:18-22 and Luke 5:27-28. What invitation does Jesus give these men who became His disciples?

5. How does that invitation add clarity to your understanding of what a disciple is?

When I was a rookie disciple, I did a word search (manually!) for every use of the word disciple in the four gospels. (I encourage you to do the same, but with an online tool such as biblegateway.com.) What left the most lasting impression on me were all the stories of the disciples following Jesus here and there. Whether He was teaching, eating, healing, or walking along the road, the disciples were following along. That image of living as a disciple still shapes how I live today, nearly thirty years later. To be a disciple is to follow where He goes. It is to live each day in His company. And to make disciples is to help other women experience that same level of intimacy with their Savior.
— SUE KLINE, AGE 58, WHITE HALL, MARYLAND

6. After following Jesus and living life with Him for a period of time, the disciples realized the seriousness of the commitment required from them. In Luke 9:23-25, Jesus describes the great impact of following Him. How does His explanation help your understanding of what a disciple is?

7. A key verb in Jesus' command is *go*. In Matthew 28:19, it can be translated, "Go, and as you are going . . ." What does that phrase tell you about the nature of making disciples?

People have been obeying Jesus' command to make disciples since the day He delivered it. Here is one woman's story of the impact on her life when someone obeyed Jesus' last words:

A woman once asked me if I knew how to know Jesus better, follow Him more closely, and look at life from His viewpoint. At first I was offended. I was so prideful that I had no idea I didn't know something I needed to know. But I had noticed how this woman served the Lord, her strong understanding of the Scriptures, and her graciousness and joy. I had none of that and I wanted it.

She proceeded to help me become a disciple of Jesus Christ. Even though we were busy with our kids (I had three and she had two, all ages four and under), we met frequently at her home, on my front steps, or at a restaurant. She arranged for some college students to babysit my children so I could meet with her — can you believe that?

Since then, I've spent my life looking for other women who are hungry and do not know what a feast they can have in Christ. They are at Christ's banquet table, and it has been my privilege to show them how to eat!
— DEB MASCHHOFF, AGE 69, MISSION VIEJO, CALIFORNIA

8. How does the woman who invited Deb to grow reflect the command of Jesus in Matthew 28?

9. Think of someone in your life who has helped you learn — maybe a teacher, friend, or coach who taught you a life skill or sport or perspective that you might not have learned on your own. What did he or she do that helped you learn?

10. How did this person let you know you were special?

11. What, if any, similarities do you see between your experience and the one Deb described in her story?

In my early twenties, I also had the privilege of being helped spiritually by another woman, but I didn't immediately make the connection that perhaps God wanted me to do the same for someone else. Then one night in the early 1970s, I was attending a prayer group. We were praying over Matthew 9:37-38 — that God would send out laborers into His harvest. I found I could not pray.

God was speaking to my heart, saying, "If you pray for others to be sent out as workers, you must be willing to be sent yourself." So while others were praying, I was confessing my fear and selfishness to God. I was agreeing with Him in prayer that I would not only pray for others to be sent out into His Harvest but also go if He would send me.

What a life-changing prayer that was. I seriously contemplated what it meant for *me* to make disciples. I had many fears and "buts" in my life at the time. I was constantly tired from caring for our first baby. Where was I supposed to find the energy and time to help another woman grow? And I wasn't skilled in making disciples; how would I ever learn? But God gently led me to trust that He could not only send me but also use me.

As you think of this command from Jesus to make disciples, you may be a lot like I was, saying, "But, Lord . . ." God is not surprised by your fears, nor is He disappointed in you for hesitating. He invites you to be honest with Him. In the next chapter, we will get real with

God and ourselves about why we feel inadequate or hesitant to follow His famous last words. Don't be fearful; you're about to enter into the most exciting adventure possible with God. And He'll be right there at your side.

CHAPTER 2

"Here Am I, Lord. Send Her!"

Suppose one of you wants to build a tower.
Will he not first sit down and estimate the cost
to see if he has enough money to complete it?
(LUKE 14:28)

She did what she could when she could.
(MARK 14:8, MSG)

I HAVE BEEN discipling women for thirty years, yet I still feel a sense of inadequacy. I know my weaknesses. And you are probably thinking, *I know mine as well.*

When I get in a funk of inadequacy, I turn to Mark 6:30-44. Maybe I identify with the circumstances: having to feed someone. I just know that this passage always encourages me. (Come to think of it, discipling others *is* a lot like feeding them.)

In Mark 6, Jesus and the disciples are seeking rest from a weighty ministry schedule. But when a crowd of five thousand assembles, Jesus sets aside His need for time off and teaches the crowd. The day grows late and people grow hungry. The disciples encourage Jesus to send the crowd away to find their own food, but Jesus says to them, "You give them something to eat." When the disciples protest, He sends them among the crowd to see what food is on hand. He then takes the five loaves of bread and two fish His disciples find, organizes the crowd, thanks His Father for providing, and tells His followers to disperse the food. What the disciples brought Him was not much and certainly not enough. But when what they had was placed under the power of Christ, it became more than enough. All five thousand were satisfied. And there were leftovers!

Can you see why I love this passage? I often feel that what I have to bring to others is not much and certainly not enough. Yet when I give God what little I have, He blesses and multiplies.

In this chapter, we'll identify the fears, hindrances, inadequacies, and concerns we might have when it comes to making disciples. Then we'll take an inventory of what assets (loaves and fish) we bring to the opportunity of making disciples and ask Jesus to bless and multiply them.

TAKING INVENTORY

1. What concerns do you have as you imagine yourself discipling other women? What makes you hesitate? Using the following list, take an inventory of your concerns. Feel free to add any concerns not included on the list.

- ☐ I am not perfect.
- ☐ I am an introvert.
- ☐ I don't have much emotional capacity.
- ☐ I don't have much relational capacity.
- ☐ I'm in a season of life (single, married, raising young children, empty nest, and so on) that's not suited to this commitment.
- ☐ I'm too hormonal.
- ☐ I have too many other priorities (husband, children, work, community, friends, extended family).
- ☐ I'm having financial problems.
- ☐ My schedule is just too full.
- ☐ I don't know the Bible well enough.
- ☐ I am too young.

☐ I am too old.

☐ I have nothing to offer.

☐ I _____ (you fill in the blank).

Even though I am a young mom, making disciples is doable for me because I'm simply passing on what I am currently learning and have already learned from others. It is less intimidating when I remember I'm just a few steps further on the journey than the women I'm helping and we can learn and grow together. The more I'm willing to share my real life with them, the more effective our discipleship times become.
— SHERRY GRAF, AGE 34, BROOKINGS, SOUTH DAKOTA

2. Do any of Sherry's comments speak to some of your fears and obstacles? If so, how?

3. How does her perspective (on finding a woman just a few steps behind her on the journey) differ from any preconceived ideas you might have held about discipling other women?

Let's step back to Mark 6 for a moment. After Jesus told the disciples to gather what food they could find, He said, "How many loaves do you have? Go and see" (verse 38). In *The Message*, "Go and see" is paraphrased "Take an inventory."

When I focus too heavily on my inadequacies, I often hear Jesus remind me, "Take an inventory." He has given all of us strengths, gifts, temperaments, and skills that He wants to bless and multiply for the benefit of the women we disciple. So we need to not only inventory what we *lack* but also identify what we *have*.

4. List here the "asset" side of your inventory. You may want to include your spiritual gifts if you know them, experiences you've had, acquired skills, and natural talents God has given you. Think about the times people have complimented you or observed a particular strength. Don't hold back; list them all.

5. You're not finished yet! Ask two or three people who know you well to give you *their* inventory of your strengths, skills, and gifts. Set aside your modesty and recognize this as an opportunity to celebrate how God made you.

6. What is the most encouraging thing you have discovered from this inventory exercise?

7. Identifying your concerns, weaknesses, and fears does not supply a reason for not making disciples! Indeed, knowing these things will give you wisdom as you choose who and how you will disciple, especially now that you have also identified your strengths and skills. Take time to pray over both your shortcomings and your strengths and give them all to Christ. Bottom line: What you have may not seem like much, but what Jesus can do with what you bring Him is always enough! Write your prayer here.

When Tom and I served in Indonesia in a campus ministry, we had three small children. I was overwhelmed by mere survival in a developing-world environment, much less stepping into the commitment to make disciples of other women. One day a missionary from a different country visited our home. I shared with him my discouragement and my sadness over my limited capacity to help others. He took me to Mark 14:1-8. Mark tells us about a woman whose name we don't know. She came to Jesus during a dinner party and made many guests furious by pouring expensive oil over Jesus' head. Jesus responded to those who were upset by saying, "She did what she could when she could" (verse 8, MSG). The question I had to answer was, "Well, then, what *can* I do?" That was different from focusing on what I thought I *should* do. So I came to the Lord and shared with Him what I had and could do. I gave it to Him. Then I poured out what I had in His name. To this day, though I still recoil at times because of my limitations, I bounce back because of this nameless woman who "did what she could when she could."

8. Take some time to read Mark 14:1-8 for yourself. Read it multiple times. Try reading it out loud a couple of times. On one of your readings, imagine the woman's perspective; on another reading, put yourself in the shoes of the indignant guests or in Jesus' shoes. Sit quietly and let the story sink into your heart. Then record here any additional insights God gives you from the passage.

9. What is one thing you learned from the Scriptures and exercises in this chapter that can help you face your fears and inadequacies as God moves you into discipling relationships with other women?

Do what you can, with what you have, where you are.
— Theodore Roosevelt

CHAPTER 3

The "B" Process

Anyone who belongs to Christ has become a new person. The old life is gone; a new life has begun! And all of this is a gift from God, who brought us back to himself through Christ. And God has given us this task of reconciling people to him.

(2 CORINTHIANS 5:17-18, NLT)

I want women I meet with (and myself)
to live in grace and truth.
— CATHY BOWMAN, AGE 59, STATE COLLEGE, PENNSYLVANIA

WE HAVE SEEN that making disciples is Christ's idea and that He empowers us and is present with us as we carry out His commission. We have also identified our fears and weaknesses related to discipling others and have surrendered them to Christ.

In this chapter, we will look more closely at what spiritual growth is—in our lives and in the lives of those we want to help grow. When I first started growing in my walk with Christ, I needed an idea of how the process of spiritual growth might unfold. Did Scripture paint a picture of some "normal" route that God has in mind for every believer? After all, we are familiar with certain stages along the way in our physical development; could similar stages or phases be identified for our new life in Christ?

You see, my experience, and my observations of others' experiences, showed me that the path to maturity was certainly not a straight line. It involved circling back at times or lingering in one "phase" much longer than in the phase before. There were detours along the path too.

I needed an illustration that would help me reconcile the reality that spiritual progress was not as simple as A plus B equals C.

The "B" Process is such an illustration. This illustration is built around the words *Before, Believe, Belong, Become,* and *Build Others.* I like this illustration because it is based on the idea that doing flows from being. In a moment, we will dig deeper into each phase of this illustration and draw some conclusions about our own growth process. First I'd like to give you an overview of the "B" Process. You'll want to refer to the chart on page 27 as you complete the discussion questions later.

HOW THE "B" PROCESS UNFOLDS

All believers have a story of what they were like **before** they invited Christ into their lives and then how they came to **believe** in Him. (We will look at this in detail in chapter 4.) Psalm 139 teaches us that even before we believe in Christ, God and evidence of His existence is all around us. But whereas before we believe, God is near us but on the outside, once we believe in Christ, God takes up residence in us through His Holy Spirit. He lives inside us.

The Scriptures teach us that the moment we trust Him by faith (believe), it is a fact that we **belong** to Him. I have found, however, after years of helping other women grow in their faith, that many are not convinced that they belong to Jesus and His family in a deep, abiding way. This missing sense of belonging inhibits their growth in Christ. Belonging to Jesus is what we are made for.

Living out of the truth that we belong to Jesus offers a refuge to run to in every season of our spiritual growth, whether we are fledgling Christians, already grounded in faith, or helping others grow. Although "belonging" is a fact, it is not often realized in our experience immediately. It is an ongoing unfolding experience through the presence of Christ as we engage in life, relationships, and circumstances.

When I received Christ into my life at the age of eleven, I put my hand in His and heard Him say, "I will never leave you or forsake you." Just as I need to know that my husband still loves me after thirty-six years of marriage, so I need to hear Christ reassure me of His love for

The B Process: The Path to Maturity

2 Corinthians 5:17

Before

You know when I sit down and when I get up. You know what I'm thinking even though you are far away. You know when I go out to work and when I come back home. You know exactly how I live. (Psalm 139:2-3, NIrV)

Believe

For me, being right with God does not come from the law. It comes because I believe in Christ. It comes from God. It is received by faith. (Philippians 3:9, NIrV)

Belong

Give praise to the God and Father of our Lord Jesus Christ. He has blessed us with every spiritual blessing. Those blessings come from the heavenly world. They belong to us because we belong to Christ. (Ephesians 1:3, NIrV)

God made us. He created us to belong to Christ Jesus. Now we can do good things. Long ago God prepared them for us to do. (Ephesians 2:10, NIrV)

Become

I am sure that the One who began a good work in you will carry it on until it is completed. (Philippians 1:6, NIrV)

Build Others

We work together with God. You are like God's field. You are like his building. God has given me the grace to lay a foundation as a master builder. Now someone else is building on it. But each one should build carefully. (1 Corinthians 3:9-10, NIrV)

He brought us back to himself through Christ's death on the cross. And he has given us the task of bringing others back to him through Christ. (2 Corinthians 5:18, NIrV)

me and His presence with me. To belong to Christ and rest in His arms is the launching place for all of my Christian life and ministry.

Our identity in Him—that we **belong** to Him—is a protective seal around us as we grow **(become)** in Christlikeness and give of our lives to **build others** in their faith. When I was in my twenties, I was learning how to make disciples. I faced several challenges: I had periods of depression, I tended toward exhaustion, and I had a temper.

As I spent time with Christ, I came to realize and trust that no matter what, I belonged to Him. And as I trusted myself to other followers of Christ who loved me also, God changed me from the inside out in these areas. The truth that I belonged to Christ was entwined with my becoming like Christ.

"Becoming" is the work that God does in us continually as we are transformed into being like Christ in character and conduct. And we respond with obedience to what God is doing, making this whole process of "becoming" a kind of partnership. Paul describes it this way in Philippians 2:12-13:

> Work hard to show the results of your salvation, obeying God with deep reverence and fear. For God is working in you, giving you the desire and the power to do what pleases him. (NLT)

Following Christ as His disciple is our work. Obeying Him daily and making godly choices toward holiness and loving God from our hearts is our work. Yet it is also God's work, for He transforms us from the inside out, giving us new desires and unmatched power to do what we would otherwise be powerless to do.

Our part in "becoming" is not working to earn points with God so He will love us more or bless us more. We already have His full blessing because we belong to Him and are unconditionally loved and accepted by Him. Rather, the work of "becoming" is to agree with God that as far as it is up to us, we will follow with our whole hearts and with obedient spirits that His Holy Spirit shows us.

"Becoming," then, launches from the platform that we belong to Christ. As this new identity of belonging sinks in, we grow in our desire

to become like Him. And as we become like Him, we grow in awareness that He has a heart for all people. He died that the world through
Him might live. As we become like Him, we begin to see the people
of the world as He sees them. We discover that He has blessed us with
gifts and abilities to be used for building others and has commissioned
us to bring others to Him and help them grow in their faith.

As I've written this workbook, I've had in mind an audience of
women who know where they came from **before** Christ, know how they
came to **believe** Christ and receive Him, are confident that they **belong**
to Him, are walking with Him and **becoming** models of growth, and
desire to see God use them to **build up** other women in their faith. My
hope is that the questions that follow will help you identify where you
are and where you want to go in confidence that God is at work in you, is
always with you, and takes great joy in seeing His children grow.

> *The greatest need that I see in the women I disciple today is the*
> *need to grow in faith and knowledge of who God is. I want them to*
> *experience hope that through the Cross, we have a better place coming.*
> *I want them to grow in love for God, themselves, and others.*
> — CATHY BOWMAN, AGE 59, STATE COLLEGE, PENNSYLVANIA

Let's look at each portion of the "B" Process. This exercise will give
you a general overview of what the women you disciple will experience
as they grow in their relationship with Christ. I believe that you will
also gain some insights into how God has been at work on your own
spiritual journey.

EXPLORING THE BEFORE PHASE
1. When was the first time you thought about God? Were your
thoughts of God positive or negative?

2. What does Psalm 139:1-18 tell you about God's involvement in your Before phase?

3. List some key words or phrases that describe the Before phase of your life.

EXPLORING THE BELIEVE PHASE

4. What brought you to the Believe phase? Identify people and events that awakened you to Christ.

Though they never said anything to me about their faith, there were two people in my student days who attracted me to Christ. Others told me that these two were "born again," which I only knew was something different from what I was. They had a peace and resolve the rest of us lacked. I finally decided it had something to do with the book my friend sometimes carried to what sounded like fun meetings in the room next door. So I got a Bible and tried to read it, but it didn't make sense. I graduated, got married, and moved across the country.

Within weeks of moving, my husband and I met a couple who invited us to investigate the Bible with them. This time it began to make sense. Eventually I had to decide if I accepted what the Bible said

*about Jesus Christ. My husband and I made that decision and told God
we wanted to be with Him and experience Christ washing away all the
gunk in our lives.*
— ANN CHRIS, AGE 55, ASIA

5. Read Philippians 3:9. What does it mean to you to believe in Christ?

EXPLORING THE BELONG PHASE

6. Read Ephesians 2:8-10. Another way to say that you belong to Christ
is that you are "in Christ." What do you understand this to mean?

7. What areas of your life have been most affected by the truth that
you are Christ's and nothing can separate you from His love?

8. Belonging to Christ also means belonging to His family, the church.
How has belonging to God's family contributed to your growth?

Even when I was still on the "outside" with Christ, I had observed a very attractive, sweet fellowship going on among the Christians around me, and I wanted to be a part of that. That was perhaps my greatest need in coming to Christ: to belong to His family. Acceptance into this new family has been so valuable to me.
— ANN CHRIS, AGE 55, ASIA

EXPLORING THE BECOME PHASE

9. Becoming like Christ is the crux of this phase. What has primarily contributed to your spiritual growth so far (personal time in the Word, sharing in a small-group Bible study, attending church, meeting one-to-one with a discipler, and so on)?

Being invited into other women's homes and lives contributed deeply to my growth. Their words were so life-giving. Along with helping me establish my personal walk with God, these women also helped me learn how to be a successful wife and mother. I was a newlywed from a somewhat dysfunctional home, so I desperately needed help in those areas.
— ANN CHRIS, AGE 55, ASIA

10. As you think about your process of "becoming," in what areas have you seen the most progress?

11. In what areas do you feel weakest?

12. Read Philippians 2:12-13 and summarize in your own words the role God plays in your becoming like Christ versus the role you play.

EXPLORING THE BUILD OTHERS PHASE

What is significant about building others is that it is something you *do*. It flows out of being strong "in Christ." As we grow in Christ, we take on the heart He has for others. Doing (building others) flows from being and not the other way around.

13. Think about the principle "Doing flows from being." Why do you think that being strong "in Christ" and becoming like Christ is essential to building others?

14. In what ways has God used others to build into your life with Him?

15. If you are reading this book, you must have some desire to help other women grow in their faith. Describe what you would like to see happen as you develop skills for discipling others.

WRAPPING IT UP

The "B" Process can be a powerful tool for helping others discern their spiritual growth lifeline and determine their future direction. After going over the "B" Process with a woman, I ask these three questions:

- Where are you?
- Where would you like to be?
- How are you going to get there?

As she identifies and explains where she sees herself for each question, I'm better able to understand where her most pressing needs for growth lie. I can cast the adventure ahead in terms of opportunity and progress in walking with Christ. And it gives the woman and me a shared language for our future meetings and evaluations.

16. What personal insights did you gain from walking through the "B" Process?

17. In what ways do you see this tool helping you as you disciple other women?

The Tools of a Discipler

NOW THAT OUR hearts have embraced Jesus' call to make disciples, it's time to acquire some tools that will help us in this process. The beauty of these tools is that they contribute to our personal spiritual growth as well.

The Navigators, an international, nondenominational ministry, developed the tools you'll encounter in this section. Staff members of The Navigators have invested in people's lives for more than seventy-five years, coming alongside them one-to-one to help them know Christ more deeply through studying the Bible, developing a deepening prayer life, sharing the faith, and memorizing and applying Scripture to daily life. In this discipling process, people are equipped to fulfill 2 Timothy 2:2—to teach others what they have learned. My husband and I have been on staff with The Navigators for more than thirty years. You can find more information about this ministry at www.navigators.org.

We are going to look at three discipling tools in depth: the testimony, the Wheel Illustration, and the Hand Illustration. At first, you may feel self-conscious using these tools. That's normal. Even a tool as simple as a hammer feels uncomfortable in your hands the first time you use it. Over time you will enjoy the freedom of adapting these tools to your own communication and discipling style.

Continued on the next page

Continued from the previous page

They will not become tools that a faceless someone told you about; they will become *your* tools. And you will find yourself using them with skill and artistry.

Chapter 4: The Testimony
Chapter 5: The Wheel Illustration
Chapter 6: The Hand Illustration

NOTE: There are other excellent discipling tools that we couldn't fit into this section. To learn more about the Bridge Illustration, Bible reading plans, *Lessons on Assurance*, and more, go to www.navigators.org and www.navpress.com. NavPress is the publishing arm of The Navigators.

The Testimony

Conduct yourselves with wisdom toward outsiders, making the most of the opportunity. Let your speech always be with grace, as though seasoned with salt, so that you will know how you should respond to each person.

(COLOSSIANS 4:5-6, NASB)

Always [be] ready to make a defense to everyone who asks you to give an account for the hope that is in you, yet with gentleness and reverence.

(1 PETER 3:15, NASB)

AS WE WALKED through the "B" Process in chapter 3, we laid some good groundwork for this first discipling tool: the testimony. To prepare your testimony, you simply describe your life before and after you trusted Christ.

I first wrote out my testimony when I was in my twenties. At the time, it seemed like a lot of work! But it was worth the effort. Because my testimony has become so familiar to me, I've been able to share it conversationally for many years, in many contexts. My brain can "download" relevant bits and pieces of my story as appropriate. I believe that your testimony will become equally valuable to you.

If the word *testimony* is intimidating, think of it this way: You are simply telling your story. Have you ever met anyone who does not enjoy hearing a good story? Set aside your need to convince or debate, and allow the simplicity of your story to speak.

But don't take my word for it. Let's see what Scripture says about the value of being able to tell our "God stories."

SETTING THE STAGE

1. Read Colossians 4:5-6 and 1 Peter 3:15-17. Both passages use the word *always*. Why do you think that word is so important in the context of telling your story?

2. What key for sharing your testimony is emphasized in the phrase "to everyone who asks you to give an account" (1 Peter 3:15, NASB)?

3. What should your attitude be as you tell your story to another person? Describe what you think that might look like in action.

4. Why do you think your attitude is important when sharing your testimony?

5. Sum up in your own words what these passages say about sharing your testimony.

WRITING YOUR TESTIMONY

To prepare your testimony—and you will do this by writing it out—you will first think through a "before," "how," and "after" section. You will then meld these three sections together. Your goal is a story you can share in roughly three minutes. That is not to say you won't sometimes tell longer or shorter versions of your testimony, but having a three-minute version handy—one you have memorized and can tell naturally—truly prepares you to "always be ready."

Here is a sample testimony to give you an idea of what you are about to write.

My Testimony

Carol Rugg, age 46, Colorado Springs, Colorado

Before

Have you ever walked around your kitchen looking for just a little something to fill that hunger in your tummy? You open the fridge and can't see anything that might hit the spot. Then you look in the pantry and the cupboards and then back to the fridge, but you can't find anything to fill your hunger. That is what my life was like before I asked Jesus to move in. I thought if I could just make one more basket or hit one more home run or raise my GPA to a 4.0 that I would feel fulfilled. But it wasn't working out that way.

One day my brother and his wife came home for a visit and told me how Jesus had changed their lives. They told me Jesus could change my life also, but I thought, *No way. I want to have fun. Asking Jesus to come into my life might be okay for later in my life but not now.*

How

I continued to seek after fulfillment through fun rather than through God. One of the fun activities I jumped at was going to Colorado for a summer trip with a youth group. Colorado was

Continued on the next page

Continued from the previous page

popular with this group because the drinking age there was eighteen. I wasn't into the drinking part, but I sure loved hiking in Colorado. At my first sight of the mountains, God began calling me toward Him. It was as if He were saying, "Look at these mountains. See how big they are? See how beautiful they are? See how creative I am? Don't be afraid of missing out on any fun if I'm around!"

Somehow I heard Him. On a quiet night by the campfire, I excused myself to be alone. I sat on a rock and asked Jesus to come into my life, fill the emptiness in my heart, and allow my hands and feet to do His work. I now know from Romans 1:20 that God speaks to all of us through His beautiful creation.

After

A month after returning home from that trip, I headed off to college. The school I had chosen was in the same town where my brother and his wife lived. They suggested I get to know God's Word, the Bible, because it could really help me understand life. So I started reading a portion of the Bible each day, and as I read, it made more and more sense to me. Then my brother and his wife introduced me to a girl who led a Bible study in my dorm, and I got involved in it — even though it met at 7:00 a.m.! I was filled with a new eagerness to learn all I could about the Lord. I even asked an upperclassman to help me learn more about Jesus. Where a nagging desire for fulfillment once existed, contentment and peace now lived.

Before

Now it's your turn! The first part of your testimony, the "before" section, briefly shares what life was like before you met Christ. If you met Christ as a kid, you might have trouble remembering what your "before" was like. I came to Christ at age eleven, and one thing I can recall is being afraid that I or my family members would die. Take your time with this part of the process and ask God to help you recall those early fears or longings that you may have since forgotten. The following questions might help you identify what's pertinent to share:

- What things were most important to you before you became a Christian?
- Where did you get your sense of security, fulfillment, and happiness?
- What did your life most revolve around?
- What fears haunted you?

Now write here a few sentences describing your life before Christ. Let's evaluate what you've written so far:

- Did you begin with an intriguing, attention-grabbing sentence?
- Can others identify with your previous lifestyle?
- Does your story have a theme (for instance, "My search for acceptance was never met")?
- Is your story interesting? Your "before" might not be dramatic (drugs, divorce, and so on), but does it at least make the listener want to know what happens next?

Make any necessary revisions to what you've written so far.

How

The second section of your testimony focuses on how you received Christ into your life. The following questions can help you crystallize your thoughts.

- How did you see these four points of the gospel play out in your life?

    Fact of sin
    Penalty of sin

Christ paid the penalty
Must receive Christ

- What was your first reaction to hearing the gospel?
- When did you first become positive about the gospel?
- What attracted you to Christ?
- What led to your decision to trust Christ?
- How did you invite Christ into your life?
- Why did you decide to give Christ complete control of your life? How did you make this decision? (These two questions are often helpful for people who placed their trust in Christ at a very young age but later made a definitive commitment to follow Him wholeheartedly.)

Now write here several sentences about how you came to place your trust in Christ. Let's evaluate what you've written for this "how" section:

- Did you avoid Christian slang (for example, *saved* and *sin*)? Many nonbelievers find these kinds of words confusing and offensive. For example, instead of saying, "I realized I was a sinner," you could say, "I realized I had fallen short of God's perfect standard."
- Did you emphasize the Bible as your authority?
- Did you use *I* and *me*, not *you*?
- Did you resist making negative comments about different churches, organizations, and people?

If you've identified changes you need to make in the "how" portion of your story, make them now.

After

The third section of your testimony is how your life changed after you trusted Christ. The following questions might help you identify some of those changes:

- How did Christ change the specific areas described in your "before" section?
- What are some specific changes in your life that illustrate what happened when you began a relationship with Christ?
- What does Christ mean to you now?

Write here a few sentences that describe your life after you placed your trust in Christ.

Now evaluate what you've written using these questions:

- Is there any clutter in your story? (One way to identify clutter is to ask, *Does this sentence move my story forward or slow it down?*)
- Can you simplify this section in any way?
- Did you use churchy words that people will not easily understand?

Make any needed revisions to your "after" section.

Many people have found this to be a very useful last line in their testimony: "The greatest benefit is that I now know I have eternal life." This statement often triggers interesting questions from the listener.

PUTTING IT ALL TOGETHER

Now it's time to combine all three sections of your testimony and see if they are coherent.

- Recite your testimony out loud. Does it sound natural? Is it how you really talk, or is it overly formal? (Many of us revert to formal college mode whenever we write.) If your testimony sounds impersonal and academic, change the language to match your conversational style.

- Continue reading your story aloud. Does it get redundant or complex in places? Do you feel the need to explain something more clearly? Just remember, if you add in one section, you might need to cut elsewhere to keep your story a reasonable length.
- Speaking of length, can you read your testimony aloud, at a natural speaking pace (not at a speed-reading pace!), in approximately three minutes?

Ask yourself these additional questions to evaluate your combined testimony:

- Are there three obvious parts: before, how, and after?
- Are transitions smooth from one part to the next?
- Did you include some human interest (your feelings, experiences, successes, humor)?
- Is it real—not overly rosy (unless that is who you are) or pat?

PRACTICE MAKES PERFECT

Once you're pleased with the written version of your testimony and have proven to yourself that it fits within the three-minute allotment, it's time to practice, practice, practice. Your goal is to become so familiar with this succinct version of your testimony that you can deliver it naturally and confidently whenever asked.

After you get the hang of it, ask a few friends to be your audience. It might feel safer to ask your Christian friends to hear your story first, but this is also a great opportunity to tell your story to someone who does not yet know Christ. Ask that person to help you decide what parts of your story are still unclear.

Have fun with this—remember, it's storytelling!

PROCESSING THE PROCESS

6. Did preparing your testimony remind you of what God has done in your life? What particularly blessed you about this process?

7. As you worked on your testimony, could you imagine yourself helping another woman through the same process? If not, what additional help would you need in order to pass this process on to someone you're discipling?

8. What do you believe are the benefits of this discipling tool?

You now have an effective tool for telling others what Christ means to you and how He has worked in your life. And you now have a process you can walk another woman through so that she too has a testimony to share. But there's another benefit I haven't mentioned yet that I want to leave you with: Whenever I review or share my testimony, I am amazed anew that God found me as He did and met me where I was, and my heart overflows with gratitude.

CHAPTER 5

The Wheel®

Illustration

Therefore as you have received Christ Jesus the Lord,
so walk in Him.

(Colossians 2:6, nasb)

WHEN I FIRST decided to follow Christ with my whole heart and mind, I knew little theology. What I did know, however, was that I was hungry to learn everything I could about Him and from Him. I had read John 17:3 — "This is eternal life: that they may know you, the only true God, and Jesus Christ, whom you have sent" — and I was exhilarated at the prospect of actually knowing Christ and having a relationship with Him.

The Wheel® Illustration provided a framework for turning my exuberance into focused, daily choices that contributed to lifelong, ever-growing intimacy and depth of relationship with Christ.

Let's walk through this illustration piece by piece, beginning with the hub.

THE HUB

Just as the driving force in a wheel comes from the hub, so the power to live the Christian life comes from Jesus Christ at the center of our lives.

The Wheel Illustration © 1976 by The Navigators, all rights reserved.

1. The apostle Paul was a man who lived with Christ at the center of his life. What did that look like for him, according to Philippians 3:10?

2. Is Paul's passion to know, love, and become like Christ different from mere belief in Christ? Why or why not?

3. What additional observations can you make from Matthew 6:31-33 and John 15:1-8 about living with Christ at the center of your life?

THE RIM

The rim on a wheel holds all the other pieces together. In this illustration, the rim represents a believer's wholehearted obedience to Christ. It's where the disciple meets the road of life.

4. Read Luke 6:46-49. Based on this passage, how would you define obedience?

5. Now read Romans 12:1-2. How does this passage add to your understanding of what it looks like to live in active obedience to Christ?

6. The very word *obedience* can sometimes evoke a grudging response on our part. We might associate it with unpleasant authority figures we have known or foolish rules we have been required to follow. But obedience to Christ is different. It comes with a promise. Read John 14:23-24. What benefits are we promised as we obey Christ?

7. Many Christians put obedience into the context of a to-do list to complete or a set of dos and don'ts to live by. Jesus puts obedience into the context of a love relationship. How does knowing this alter the way you've been thinking about obedience?

THE SPOKES

In order for a wheel to travel smoothly and without hindrance, the length of its spokes must be balanced: equal in length and strength. The spokes in The Wheel® Illustration are areas of spiritual growth that thrive best when they are in balance.

Before we continue, however, I want to issue a caution. We all live slightly off balance, don't we? Maybe you're well prepared for Bible study but your house is a disaster area. You're caught up at work but haven't gone to your Pilates class for six months. Your relationship with your parents has never been better, but you've ticked off your neighbor. And so on.

It can be that way with the spokes we are about to look at. Sometimes your wiring comes into play: As an extrovert, you may have many rich relationships with other believers that keep your "fellowship spoke" strong, but you struggle with sitting still and praying.

Seasons of life also affect the strength of your spokes. Time spent in the Word and prayer may look different when you are a new mom. I was so tired after our first child was born! However, I did find ways to meet with the Lord, even if not as frequently or for as long as during my pre-parenting days. Sometimes as soon as I'd put our baby down for a nap, I'd turn to my Bible (and, yes, sometimes I'd fall asleep shortly afterward). Or I would tape a favorite Bible verse over the kitchen sink and meditate on it as I cleaned the dishes. If you have recently moved to a new town, that too can affect the quality of your spokes. For instance, you may lack fellowship for a time while you find and settle into a new church or small group.

You will probably feel healthiest spiritually when all four spokes are strong. But don't obsess. Allow for seasons, for the personality God gave you, for interference from life crises, and so on. And always bear in mind that the spokes are not about looking good or completing a checklist; they're about growing in your knowledge of and love for God and your capacity to receive and enjoy *His* love (and then showing someone else how to do the same!).

Now to the spokes. The vertical spokes in The Wheel® Illustration represent our relationship with God and His relationship with us through the Word and prayer. The horizontal spokes represent our relationship with people through fellowship and witnessing.

THE VERTICAL SPOKES: THE SCRIPTURES

God has chosen to speak to us through His written Word, the Bible. It is key to our relationship with Him, as Hannah Hanneman, age 33, of Boulder, Colorado, explains:

> I didn't know how to have an intimate relationship with my Savior. I needed help from day one. The two things that helped me most when I was being discipled were learning how to memorize and apply Scripture to my life, and learning and believing the promises of God. I saw the passion for both in my discipler's life, and it was contagious. Through the Scriptures, God gripped my heart with the same passions, and they continue to this day.

8. What do these verses tell you about why the Scriptures are essential in the life of a follower of Christ?

a. Joshua 1:8

b. 2 Timothy 3:16

9. Read 2 Kings 23:1-3. What did King Josiah commit to doing?

10. Notice the role of the heart in Josiah's response to the Scriptures. Now read Ezra 7:10. What role does our heart play as we spend time in the Scriptures?

11. What does Isaiah 66:2 reveal about the heart response God desires from us?

12. What do you think it means to tremble at His Word?

In the next chapter, we will look in depth at ways we can make the most of our times in God's Word.

THE VERTICAL SPOKES: PRAYER

While God speaks to us through His Word, we talk to Him through prayer, which is the second vertical spoke in The Wheel® Illustration.

13. Prayer is conversation with God. Why are good conversations so essential to good relationships?

14. Sitting in a coffee shop talking with a friend you can see, hear, and touch seems very different from praying to an invisible God. Yet the Bible assures us that God is not just a distant observer of our prayers; He is a participant. What do these verses say about God's response to your prayers?

    a. Jeremiah 33:3

    b. John 14:14

    c. John 15:7

d. Philippians 4:6-7

THE HORIZONTAL SPOKES: FELLOWSHIP

True fellowship is more than attending church; it is having regular, active relationships with other believers that center on Christ, His Word, and prayer. True fellowship provides Christians with mutual care, encouragement, accountability, and a sense of shared purpose.

15. How does Hebrews 10:24-25 describe the kind of relationship believers should have with one another?

16. How has your experience of fellowship spurred you on to knowing Christ better?

17. The writer of Hebrews warns against giving up meeting with other Christians. Why is doing so not healthy?

18. In his letter to the young church at Ephesus, Paul described various relational dynamics of fellowship. Read Ephesians 4:25-32 and list here what fellowship should—and should not—look like.

THE HORIZONTAL SPOKES: WITNESSING

Witnessing is sharing Christ through our lives, words, and deeds as we relate to those who don't yet have a relationship with Him. Jesus spoke of our role as witnesses in Acts 1:8 when He said to His followers, "You will be my witnesses . . . to the ends of the earth."

19. In Matthew 4, Jesus invites Peter, Andrew, James, and John to follow Him—that is, to be His disciples. In verse 19, what does Jesus promise to do for them?

20. What do you think Jesus means by "fishers of men"?

21. Acts 4 describes a witnessing experience involving two of the men Jesus called in Matthew 4, Peter and John. Read verses 1-13. What did the authorities conclude about these two disciples (see verse 13)?

22. Although Peter and John were ordinary men—former fishermen—they stood out in the crowd because they had "been with Jesus." What do you think it looks like today to be someone who has "been with Jesus"?

23. The disciples' effectiveness in witnessing was the result of, in part, the evidence of Jesus in their lives. Another key to their witnessing lay in the power of their message. What do the following verses tell you about the message we are called to proclaim?

   a. Romans 1:16

   b. Romans 5:8-9

   c. 1 Corinthians 15:1-4

d. 1 John 5:11-12

24. Read Romans 10:14-15. Why is it important to have relationship with nonbelievers?

USING THE WHEEL® ILLUSTRATION

25. How effective do you think The Wheel® Illustration might be for evaluating growth and balance in *your* spiritual life?

26. How might The Wheel® Illustration help you disciple others?

Read these words from a young woman who has been using The Wheel® Illustration in her discipling ministry:

As I began to develop my toolbox for discipling others, I realized that the most important lessons and skills I wanted to pass along were encompassed by The Wheel Illustration. I take each part of The Wheel and design lesson plans based on where that particular woman is in her spiritual maturity. For example, if I want to help a woman grow in prayer, we might begin by studying the Lord's Prayer and learning

how Jesus taught His disciples to pray. Then I might teach her how to pray through Scripture or how to do a prayer walk. Over time I will do something similar with each element of the Wheel, and then she'll have her own tools (pertaining to keeping Christ the center of her life, obeying Him, being in the Word, praying, witnessing, and fellowship) that will help her walk with the Lord for a lifetime.
— STACY FRAZER, AGE 28, BOULDER, COLORADO

27. To further reinforce the elements in The Wheel® Illustration, try filling in this blank wheel. Are there some things you'd like to word differently? Feel free! This is a tool; adapt it so that it's comfortable for you to use.

CHAPTER 6

The Hand™

Illustration

*"So Jesus was saying to those Jews who had believed Him,
"If you continue in My word, then you are truly
disciples of Mine; and you will know the truth,
and the truth will make you free."*
(JOHN 8:31-32, NASB)

IN THE WHEEL® Illustration, we saw that the Word of God is one of the "spokes" essential to a growing relationship with Christ. For me, spending time with Jesus in His Word has been *the* most essential and exciting ingredient for deepening my relationship with Him.

The Hand™ Illustration shows us how to engage with God's Word. I remember the first time I saw this illustration. I was excited that there were so many options for encountering God in the Scriptures. I wanted to know His ways and His thoughts. And I wanted my heart and mind to take on His ways and thoughts so that I could live wisely. I have found over time that I have not always lived perfectly but I've always had God's guidance and help through His Word.

The Hand™ Illustration presents five ways we can spend time in the Scriptures, one method per finger. As we regularly include these methods in our pursuit of God's Word, we will eventually acquire a good grasp of the Bible. We will grow in understanding what Christ thinks, who He is, and how much He desires a relationship with us.

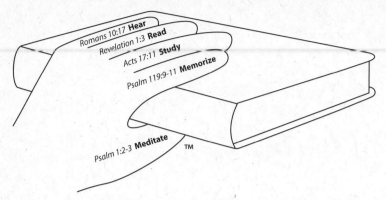

Romans 10:17 **Hear**
Revelation 1:3 **Read**
Acts 17:11 **Study**
Psalm 119:9-11 **Memorize**

Psalm 1:2-3 **Meditate** ™

HEARING THE WORD

Hearing is the easiest way of taking in Scripture. As we hear the Word from godly pastors and teachers, we benefit from others' studies of the Scriptures, and our appetite for God's Word is stimulated. Hearing can occur at church, at conferences, or while listening to the radio, CDs, and podcasts. While hearing the Word is helpful, if we only listen to others share the Word without other means of intake, we will not experience the wonder of finding God's truth for us in a personal way. Hearing is a passive rather than active way of engaging with Scripture.

1. Why is hearing the Word of God important (see Romans 10:17; James 1:22-25)?

2. Hearing the Word is represented by the pinky, the weakest finger. Why do you think this is so?

READING THE WORD

Reading the Bible gives an overall picture of God's Word. Many people find it helpful to use a daily reading program that takes them systematically through the Bible. Many such plans are available online.

Systematically moving through the entire Bible is not the only way to read it. Sometimes you'll just want to sit down and read a passage in the Bible without any reason other than to know Christ better.

3. In Deuteronomy 17, God predicts that the nation of Israel will want a king once they enter the Promised Land. Read verses 18-20. What did God want any king who was selected to do daily?

4. These verses describe some specific purposes for daily Bible reading. What are they?

5. How does this motivate you to read the Bible consistently?

STUDYING THE WORD

Studying the Scriptures is different from studying any other book. The Word of God is alive and powerful. It is God's personal revelation to us. Bible study can lead to a deeper, personal understanding of who God is. It also helps us grow in godly wisdom. Studying the Word is not just about gaining head knowledge (that is, acquiring facts and principles), although that type of knowledge does have value. God's desired outcome for our study is that we deepen our intimacy with Him in a way that transforms our character.

Bible study can be based on a biblical character, topic, or book. As we write down discoveries about God's character and purposes revealed in the Scriptures, we retain more of what we learn.

6. Read Hebrews 4:12-13. How is the Bible different from any other book?

7. Proverbs 2:1-5 urges a particular approach to Scripture. List here the phrases used by the author to describe how you should study God's Word.

8. In what ways is studying the Word like searching for hidden treasure?

9. Why are the Bereans in Acts 17:11 commended?

10. Summarize how studying Scripture is different from reading it.

MEMORIZING THE WORD

The index finger is the finger we use most from day to day. In The Hand™ Illustration, it represents memorizing the Word. Scripture memory is a vital way to take Scripture into our lives. It allows us to engage with God's Word wherever we are, whatever we are doing. When we know the Scriptures by heart, we have the help at hand to strengthen our spirits as we walk through daily circumstances and relationships, we have the Sword of the Spirit to overcome Satan and temptations, and we can more effectively share our faith with nonbelievers or offer wise counsel.

11. Describe your experience up to this point in memorizing Scripture.

12. Describe a time when a verse or passage you had memorized from the Bible helped you in some way.

13. What benefits of memorizing Scripture do you find in these verses?

a. Psalm 119:9,11

b. Proverbs 7:1-3

c. Colossians 3:16

One tool available from The Navigators that especially helped me to memorize Scripture is the Topical Memory System (TMS). It includes sixty foundational verses and instructions on how to memorize them. As I learned these verses, I began incorporating them into my testimony, using them to fight temptation, sharing them with other women who wanted a richer relationship with Jesus, and so on. Today I continue to draw on those first sixty verses I memorized. You can learn more about the TMS at www.navpress.com.

MEDITATING ON THE WORD

Meditation is represented by the thumb. It's hard to grasp anything well without a thumb. In the same way, we cannot get a good grasp of the Word of God without meditation.

Most dictionaries define meditation as continued or extended thought, reflection, and contemplation. It involves mentally chewing over something you've just read or heard. In fact, the act of meditation is often compared to the way cows chew their cud.

14. What reasons do the following verses give for meditating on Scripture?

a. Joshua 1:8

b. Psalm 1

c. Psalm 19:7-14

d. Jeremiah 15:16

15. Which of the reasons most motivates you?

Perhaps the biggest obstacle to meditating on Scripture is not knowing how to begin. Here are a few ways to ponder a passage slowly and thoughtfully:

- Use basic reporters' questions—who, what, where, when, why, and how—to uncover how a passage relates to your life.
- Read a verse multiple times, emphasizing a different word each time. Then consider what stood out to you from this exercise.
- Pray over a verse phrase by phrase. For each phrase, ask God what He wants to impress upon you.

Prayer is vitally linked to meditation. As you meditate on God's Word in silence—and as you talk to God about what you're noticing in the passage you're meditating on—it is His still, small voice you want to hear. He may show you a change He wants you to make. He may give you a fresh glimpse of His character. He may offer guidance for a problem you've been trying to solve. He may simply speak of His love for you. Through the practice of meditation, we quiet ourselves sufficiently to hear from God in ways we might not amid our usual hectic schedules.

HOW'S YOUR HAND?

16. List here the five ways you just learned for making God's Word a part of your life.

17. Which of your "fingers" is strongest?

18. Which is weakest — or maybe missing altogether?

19. What is one way you could strengthen that weak finger?

20. Now that you have walked through The Hand Illustration and applied it to your life, how might you use it to help another woman develop deeper intimacy with Christ through her engagement with His Word?

One way many women apply the principles in The Hand Illustration is through daily devotions, or a "quiet time." Here's how Beth Luebe describes her practice of daily time in God's Word:

> *Jesus said, "I am the bread of life" (John 6:35). His Word, the Bible, is my daily bread for soul nourishment and health. It's the way I best connect with God and hear from Him. Often we rely on a weekly sermon for our spiritual nourishment. The rest of the week, our Bibles lie on the nightstand, untouched. But I've found that I can't survive on a once-a-week meal if I want to be well nourished. I need to go to God's Word daily to meet with Him, to learn of Him, and to seek His ways for my life. Time in God's Word daily keeps my relationship with Jesus healthy and vibrant.*
> — BETH LUEBE, AGE 46, COLORADO SPRINGS, COLORADO

There is no right or wrong way to have this daily time with God. Listen to this woman's description of how she meets with God:

> *I rather resist talking about "time with God" as if it's limited to fifteen minutes every morning. As I grow in trust and intimacy with God, I've learned that every minute of every day is time with Him! But I do always carve out anywhere from ten to thirty minutes each day that I think of as "just God and me" time. Most days I read a short passage of Scripture and talk it over with God. Occasionally I will write down something God impresses upon me or I'll choose a verse to memorize. Some days I just talk to God about a burden I'm carrying or a fear I'm fighting. He almost always brings a verse to mind that sustains me for the rest of the day (that's a plug for memorizing Scripture!). On especially crazy days, I'll sing worship songs to God while I pull the house together or get myself ready for work. There's no finger in the Hand Illustration for singing Scripture, but it's another great way to fill my life with God's Word and His presence.*
> — SUE KLINE, AGE 58, WHITE HALL, MARYLAND

From the stories of these two women and your recent exploration of The Hand Illustration, several possible ingredients of a daily time with God and His Word may have come into focus. I've listed them—and a few others—here. Pick and choose to your heart's delight. This is not a legalistic activity that you must complete in order to gain God's favor; it is simply another way to deepen and sweeten your relationship with Christ through meeting Him in His Word.

- Quieting yourself before God
- Having a conversation with Him
- Reading and meditating on His Word
- Asking Him to speak to you about what you've read
- Writing down things that stand out to you
- Reviewing favorite verses that have been foundational to your walk of faith
- Praying for people God brings to mind
- Offering Him praise and thanksgiving, in prayer or in singing

If you aren't currently meeting with God each day for some "just us" time, why not start tomorrow? Write here a time and place where you can spend a few minutes with your Bible and your heavenly Father.

You may be regularly having quiet times, but it might not have occurred to you to teach another woman how to do the same thing. Write here the name of a woman you know who would benefit from hearing how you spend time with God each day. Make a date with her this week if at all possible.

The Skills of a Discipler

EVEN THOUGH YOU are now armed with such tools as your testimony, The Wheel Illustration, and The Hand Illustration, you still have questions, right? *Who am I supposed to help? What do I share with her when we meet? Do I need a plan, or do I wing it? What does all this look like?*

In this section, you will acquire skills as a discipler. You will hear from a variety of women who've been discipling others for years. They started at the beginning, just like you. The skills they will describe weren't always natural to them, just as tennis and sewing and text messaging are not natural when you first start doing them. But over time these women added their own touches and personalities to their discipling skills and acquired a real artistry in their personal ministry. The same will happen with you.

CHAPTER 7

Who Do I Help?

The things which you have heard from me in the presence of
many witnesses, entrust these to faithful men who will be able
to teach others also.

(2 TIMOTHY 2:2, NASB)

YOU ARE NOW equipped with some great tools to pass along to other women who want to grow a deep relationship with Christ. But where do you find these women? Discipling another woman is an investment of your time and your life. It is not merely the occasional cup of coffee with someone. As with any investment, you want to invest in the right place—or, in this case, the right women.

Let's let a few experienced disciplers speak to this issue.

Who do I disciple? First of all I pray that God will give me a FAT woman—that is, Faithful, Available, and Teachable. Then I put my feelers out. I listen to women answer questions in Bible study. In conversation with them, I gauge whether they seem eager to know God better or whether they pull back when I talk about spiritual things. As I meet young women at church and a particular woman frequently crosses my path, I'll ask her if anyone has ever shown her how to meet with the Lord daily. That's where I begin. When I asked one woman about this a few years ago, she said, "Are you asking to disciple me? This happened to my sister and I have been praying it would happen to me!" I ended up discipling this woman, and she is now discipling her third woman.

— GRETCHEN RIEDEL, AGE 72, FONTANA, WISCONSIN

Meaghan started coming to my Bible study her sophomore year of college. I quickly saw that she was looking forward to growing in her relationship with Christ, was faithful, and had a heart for God and people. She and I started meeting regularly at a coffee shop and had devotions together, talked about life, spent time in God's Word, and prayed together. We discussed how she could be a light for Jesus on her campus and grow in intimacy with Jesus. When Meaghan started to lead a Bible study and meet one-to-one with a freshman in her study, I gave her tools and ideas.
—Lori Butler, age 28, Tuscon, Arizona

As I lead a Bible study, I pray for a discipling relationship with one or two women in the group. I want God to use me in another woman's life the way He used Lori in mine.
—Meaghan Hart, age 23, Colorado Springs, Colorado

1. What role does prayer play in the stories you just read?

2. Read Luke 6:12-13. How is Christ a model for you as you begin to seek women to disciple?

3. What does 1 Samuel 16:7 tell you about the qualities to look for in the women you disciple?

4. What are some things a woman might do or say that indicate she has a heart to grow in Christ?

5. In 2 Timothy 2:2, how does Paul describe the kind of men he wants Timothy to invest in?

6. Read Proverbs 20:6. What does it say about a faithful person?

7. Think of someone you'd describe as faithful. What is it about her actions or attitudes that leads you to describe her that way?

8. At the beginning of this chapter, Gretchen referred to FAT women: faithful, available, and teachable. We've looked at faithfulness. Now let's look at the "A." What qualities make a woman available?

Sometimes availability has more to do with heart attitude than scheduling. A busy career woman with a family may seem like a poor candidate for availability, yet you may find she will readily make time for anything that will help her grow closer to Christ. Conversely, if you begin to help a woman who seems to have time on her hands but repeatedly misses your get-togethers or comes unprepared, you may be dealing with someone who is not truly available in her heart.

9. The last part of FAT is "teachable." Read Proverbs 19:20. According to this verse, what qualities are present in a teachable woman?

10. What does James 1:22-25 tell you about why teachability is so critical to spiritual growth?

11. How has reading these women's stories in this chapter and reading the relevant verses helped you clarify who you want to disciple?

Remember the role we saw prayer playing in the stories in the beginning of this chapter? Set aside time each day for the next few weeks to ask God to show you the FAT woman He wants you to disciple.

"I'VE FOUND HER. NOW WHAT?"

Let's say someone has either sought you out for help or you've noticed someone with a hunger to grow. What do you do next? Here are some tips for starting well.

Agree on why you are meeting. Do not begin without agreeing on why you are meeting together. You both must have clarity on where you are and where you are headed. When a woman asks me to meet with her, I normally say, "Let me pray about this." I also ask her to think through what she is hoping for if we meet together. Then we set up a time in the near future to talk through her desires and needs. Before I agree to meet on a regular basis, I want to identify two things: What is she asking for, and can I help her with what she is seeking? When it seems clear our expectations are mutual, we move forward.

Clear up details before you begin. Answer such questions as, How often will we meet? Where will we meet? Will there be assignments? For how long a period of time will we meet? How will we evaluate our get-togethers? How will we know if it's time to stop?

There are no right and wrong answers to these questions. Some women meet weekly; some meet monthly. Some meet for an hour; others find they need more time. Some meet outside the home, and others meet in the kitchen. Hear are variations from some of the disciplers I know:

I met weekly with two girls from my Bible study for a year. It began with my inviting them for coffee and getting to know them. Then we began meeting every week to pray together and spend time in the Word.
— MEAGHAN HART, AGE 23, COLORADO SPRINGS, COLORADO

Discipleship looks a bit different for me now that I have two children. Mostly we meet in my home. The other young women and I talk and pray in the midst of changing diapers, training children, and serving my family. These women want tools for ministry and someone to process things with, but they also desire to just be with me in real-life situations and see me interact with and serve my family. They want to see what a home and family is like that's striving to have Jesus at the center. They can see that when I allow them into my world.
— HEATHER HANNEMAN, AGE 33, BOULDER, COLORADO

I try not to enter a discipling relationship without an initial trial period. I simply suggest we meet together once a week for the next month and then evaluate whether we'd like to continue.
— KIM HAVENSTEIN, AGE 37, LINCOLN, NEBRASKA

*We aim to meet at night when the husbands can watch the kids
or during naps. Sometimes we need to relax our goals for the time
because of the kids; if we're not flexible, we can easily get frustrated.
Sometimes the children become an object lesson themselves!*
— ELLEN SUSMAN, AGE 43, COLORADO SPRINGS, COLORADO

*When I was first discipled, I was a busy career woman and so was my
discipler. We met at least once a week, but it looked very different from
one week to the next. Sometimes we talked together while running
errands. Sometimes we met early in the morning before work or at
night after our group Bible study ended. She discipled me in the car, in
the laundry room while we folded, and while weeding flower beds. All
that mattered to me was that I was with her and we were focused on
Christ and His Word.*
— SUE KLINE, AGE 58, WHITE HALL, MARYLAND

As you can see, you can determine the details of your discipling
relationship based on whatever season of life you are in.

*Determine the degree of permission you have to speak into another
person's life.* This is another detail to define early. You need to ask the
woman you plan to disciple, "Will I be able to tell you what I think you
need? How would you feel if I spoke to some weaknesses or difficulties?"

*At the beginning of a discipling relationship, when we're sharing what
we hope for and expect from the time, I often ask if she would like the
type of friendship where we will feel free to speak into each other's
lives if we see anything inconsistent with Scripture. Everyone I've
ever asked about that has been very eager. It's such a huge blessing to
identify that up front because later, when an issue arises that I feel the
Holy Spirit is prompting me to bring up, I'm able to say, "Remember
when we said that we wanted to speak into each other's lives? Is that
still true? Because there's something I've noticed that I just want
to mention, and then you can ask the Lord if there's anything there
that He wants you to consider." I think that's what asking permission
means.*
— KIM HAVENSTEIN, AGE 37, LINCOLN, NEBRASKA

Pray and begin. When you have confidence that this person is ready for relationship with you for the purpose of her growth, then begin.

KNOW YOUR LIMITS

There's one last consideration for women who want to disciple women: You need to know your own limitations. Some people can meet with one woman a week, some with two a week. Some operate best by meeting every other week.

I recommend that you start with one woman and meet either weekly or biweekly. Over time, if your life stage and other time commitments allow, you may want to start meeting with additional FAT women. Don't put pressure on yourself, however, to do more than God leads you to do. Here are some words from a long-time discipler:

> Sometimes I find myself holding back from engaging in conversations about discipling women. Why? Because I cannot offer to meet with anyone else due to my own time constraints. I find that two or possibly three women is my limit, especially if I want to leave time for teaching Bible studies, which I also love doing.
> — GRETCHEN RIEDEL, AGE 72, FONTANA, WISCONSIN

As in every step of becoming a discipler, ask God for guidance and then listen to what He tells you. Just as you can trust Him to lead you to the right women, you can also trust Him to show you your reasonable limits.

CHAPTER 8

What Do I Share?

*Go and make disciples . . . teaching them
to obey everything I have commanded you.*
(MATTHEW 28:19-20)

ONCE YOU'VE MET a woman who wants you to help her grow in Christ, the next question to enter your mind is sure to be, *What do I share with her?* You aren't alone in asking this question.

> *My greatest challenge in beginning to disciple a woman is where to start. Has she ever opened the Bible before? Does she know what a quiet time is, and is she having one? Is she witnessing to others, or does she not quite understand the gospel for herself? I always want to teach her everything all at once, and I have a hard time deciding the most important place to start. It always feels as if there is so much to cover and so little time.*
> — STACY FRAZER, AGE 28, BOULDER, COLORADO

Every person who knows Christ will experience transformation. It will look unique to each person, and this is part of the challenge of knowing where to begin and what to pass along to another person. But though we are each unique, there are general stages of growth in Christ that tend to be common to all of us. As we understand what these stages are and the needs associated with each stage, we find the answers we need to our question "What do I share?"

1. For some insight into the stages of spiritual growth, let's look at 1 John 2:12-14. What three levels of maturity does John describe in this passage?

2. Do you remember the "B" Process from chapter 3? In what ways do these levels of maturity in 1 John 2 correspond to the "B" Process?

The Lifeline Illustration that I'm about to show you combines the "B" Process with a general overview of topics a person might cover in each phase of that process. This illustration is not a "required reading" list of topics to be covered with every woman you disciple; rather, it is a compilation of *possible* topics to cover with the women you disciple. Use it as a guideline as you discern — with God's help — what topics are best suited to the women you are helping. You may notice that I have not included topics for the "before" and "believe" phase. This is because during these two phases individuals are transitioning toward trusting Christ. During these phases, though intentional as I relate to a person, I am connecting with them informally. Again, the purpose of the Lifeline Illustration is to stimulate you to think through what everyone who believes should know from the Word as they move forward in growth.

During the Belong phase in a disciple's life, we want to lay a foundation of the Word of God. We major on basics such as the gospel message, the importance of Scripture and prayer in a believer's growth, and the love and forgiveness of God.

During the Become phase, we build upon those basics and broaden a woman's scope. In his book *The Lost Art of Disciplemaking*, Leroy Eims describes the phase this way: "You want to see [her] go from taking in spiritual milk to partaking of spiritual meat." We take her deeper into the Word through study and explore how to apply biblical truth to everyday issues.

The Lifeline Illustration

PHASE	TOPICS
Belong:	Assurance of Salvation
	God's Love
	Quiet Time*
	Prayer*
	Identity in Christ
	Sharing Christ with Others (your testimony)
	God's Forgiveness
	The WORD is your LIFE (Sample Package in chapter 9) * Some women use the Hand and/or Wheel Illustrations with these topics
Become:	Doctrinal Studies (such as God's attributes)
	Character Studies (such as Deborah, Rahab, Mary, Sarah)
	Book Studies (such as Ruth, Colossians, Ephesians, Philippians)
	Living by Faith
	Men/Women Relationships
	Spiritual Warfare
Build Others:	Discipling Women
	World Vision
	Ministry Skills
	Lifetime Laboring
	Christ's Return
	Spiritual Gifts

The Build Others phase is where we help women learn to help others. The focus is on training them as laborers for Christ. While my husband and I were missionaries in Indonesia for more than ten years, I noticed that women missionaries who were most spiritually agile and engaged in ministry had built strong foundations in the basics in the Belong and Become phases. They owned a personal vision for how they were called to serve God, and they had the spiritual stamina and skills required for laboring, whatever the stresses and challenges.

Ultimately we hope to see every woman become strong in the Build Others phase, though we might not be the ones to guide them into that phase. I have rarely taken someone all the way from Believe to Build Others; more often I am a link in the chain of a woman's journey. Understanding and accepting this reality frees me to engage with women where they are in their growth for as long as God gives us.

I cannot stress enough that the Lifeline Illustration is a tool to help you make your own plan with whomever you're helping. It is not a one-size-fits-all outline, but it does help to bring intentionality to one's discipling. As you get to know the woman you're discipling, topics will emerge that aren't even mentioned in the Lifeline Illustration. As mentioned earlier, spiritual growth is rarely linear. The woman you disciple may have needs that push you to cover content from both the Belong and Become phases (depending on her life circumstances), old issues that surface, or simply the need to reinforce certain basic truths from time to time.

With all this in mind, here are some questions you can ask to get the most out of the Lifeline Illustration without becoming a slave to it:

- What topics do you remember having been vital for your spiritual growth when you first began to follow Christ?
- What topics on this Lifeline, if any, did you miss studying in your personal investigation of the Word?
- On what topics have you memorized verses? Are those topics on this list, or do you need to add them?
- What are some "must have" topics that come to mind that are not on this list? In your opinion, why are those topics essential?

Now, keeping a specific woman in mind whom you are discipling (or whom you hope to disciple), use the Lifeline Illustration and your own reflections to create a customized plan for topics to cover when you meet. Try to list six to eight topics per category.

BELONG	BECOME	BUILD OTHERS

Having a plan helps me in my discipleship relationships. It is inevitable that, on occasion, I come to a one-to-one appointment where life's difficulties and disappointments override my plan. However, I always try to come with something prepared for us to do together. I have found that the women I disciple are grateful for a plan and feel honored that I would think through their needs and what will help them grow.

— STACY FRAZER, AGE 28, BOULDER, COLORADO

THE ROLE OF THE HOLY SPIRIT

Some of us will find it daunting to "engineer" a plan for a person's life. In truth, we are simply equipping ourselves with tools and methods that will help us respond to what the Holy Spirit is already doing in a woman's life. The Lifeline exists to stimulate us as we think and pray over others' needs. As you talk to God about an upcoming appointment with a woman you're discipling, you may want to pray something along these lines:

> Lord, I know You are at work in [Christy's] life. Your Holy Spirit is already transforming her into the woman You want her to be. Show me what role I can play in that transformation this week. Is there a topic in the Lifeline that I should cover with her? Is there a struggle in her life that You want me to address? As I prepare now for my time with [Christy], guide my thinking. Show me the best topic to cover with her this week.

This story from an experienced discipler shows the balance between planning ahead and responding to the Holy Spirit:

> It is certainly wise to discern a disciple's needs prior to a one-to-one meeting, think through how to move her forward in that area through your time together, and direct the conversation in that direction. But you don't want to gaze so intently on your plan that you can't see a more immediate need when it surfaces. Be led by the Spirit, open to changing your plan to fit His plan.
>
> One day last year I was preparing to meet with a particular girl I'd been helping. As usual I had protected some time to think through her spiritual needs and discern which would be good to discuss in our time together. Recently a sin had risen to the surface in her life, and I felt this would be a good time to address it with her. I did my homework, looked up Scriptures to share with her, made my list of observations, and reminded myself of how to approach a tricky subject like this one. I even carried into the meeting a piece of paper in my back pocket with my list of observations and Scriptures in case I needed to refer to them.
>
> As soon as we began to talk, however, it was apparent that something was wrong. She revealed that some trust issues were resurfacing and were overwhelming her. She felt that everyone was against her and she could trust no one. At that moment, I knew that

the list I had made needed to stay in my back pocket that day. It would do no good to bring up the sin I had observed in her life when she was already unsure if anyone was for her.

The conversation went a very different direction from what I had planned that day, but it went the way it needed to go. The time to address her sin would come later. Since that experience, I often refer to "keeping my plan in my back pocket." A discipler needs to be wise enough to have a plan in her back pocket as well as discerning enough to leave it there when it is appropriate to do so. "A man's heart plans his way, but the LORD directs his steps" (Proverbs 16:9, NKJV).

— MELANIE ROGERS, AGE 31, LAFAYETTE, LOUISIANA

In the next chapter, you'll discover how the Lifeline Illustration can help you develop a library of content that you can share with women throughout a lifetime.

CHAPTER 9

How Do I Prepare?

*What you heard from me, keep as the pattern of sound teach-
ing, with faith and love in Christ Jesus.*
(2 TIMOTHY 1:13)

*Do your best to present yourself to God as one approved,
a workman who does not need to be ashamed and
who correctly handles the word of truth.*
(2 TIMOTHY 2:15)

IN CHAPTER 7, we learned how to identify FAT women to invest in.
Then in chapter 8, we learned the kinds of topics we want to pass along
to these women. Now we're ready to see how to prepare our minds and
hearts for meeting with the women we're discipling.

During my twenties, when I was learning how to disciple women,
I was challenged to create "packages" for each topic I wanted to share
with another woman. This appealed to me. I saw a package as a gift I
would give her, like a present I'd give someone for her birthday. I would
not give a friend just any old thing as a gift. I would think about her
personality, her loves, and her needs. The same things motivated me in
creating discipling packages.

What a huge help this was to me! First I grew personally as I dug
into the Scriptures and created content that came from my personal
study and my life and not someone else's book. It was not my bent to do
this kind of work, yet the blessings far outweighed the time and effort
it took. Eventually I had a thick notebook of packages I had created.

The packages I created back then gave me confidence when I met with women who wanted to be discipled. My goal was to become so agile and wise on a topic that I would outgrow my need for packaged content. Now, thirty-five years later, I meet with women without my notebook full of "packages" because that content has become such a part of who I am. Still I am thankful I did all that work in my early days of discipling.

A package is a short, simple lesson on a selected topic from Scripture. Though the focus of the package is on what the Bible teaches, a package should also include your personal experience with the topic. And it needs to be relevant to the life of the woman you are discipling. Making your package relevant is like wrapping a gift in just the right paper and bow. It goes back to what I said earlier about how I love finding the perfect gift for a friend. When the package is relevant, even the wrapping is just right.

Before I start describing the process of creating a discipling package, I want to stress a few things that you might have breezed by in the previous paragraphs. First, unless you are a natural and avid student, these packages can be daunting to prepare. Please don't let that discourage you from at least giving it a try.

Second, the preparation and use of these packages may be just for a season. Think of this as your studies required to get a degree and acquire proficiency. The day may come when you won't even refer to your packages any longer. Yet without them, you may never take that first step toward discipling another woman, if for no other reason than you lack confidence.

And finally, let me stress that women have discipled other women for eons without having nice, neat lessons in hand. Packages are tools intended to make discipling more doable but never intended to replace what really matters: the meeting of two women's hearts over a shared desire to grow in love for and obedience to Christ.

I invite you to walk through this process with me, create at least one package for yourself using the guidelines in this chapter, use that package with a woman you are helping, and then evaluate. If the process was fun, as it was for me long ago, then keep at it with other topics. If the process was dreary and you are good at pulling from your heart and mind applicable verses and life stories on many of your discipling topics, then set aside this tool as not particularly useful and move on.

Here are some things to do before you write a package:

- Choose a topic and then do a Bible study on the topic. A concordance and study Bible are huge helps in this process.
- After you've looked up relevant verses, ask yourself, *What verses communicate most clearly on this topic? What verses motivate me in this area? What verses best explain how to practice this topic?*
- Choose the five clearest, most motivating verses to be your core verses.
- Whenever possible, choose at least one passage from the teaching of Jesus. For example, if you are preparing a package on prayer, you may want to use Luke 11:1-4.

Each package might contain the following elements: an objective, an introduction, motivation, a plan, examples/illustrations, assignments/resources, and a progress check.

- **Objective:** Begin with a short, clear objective of what you hope to accomplish. For example, "To help Elisa to begin praying regularly."
- **Introduction:** How will you introduce the topic? There are many ways to do so. You can ask a question, ask for her definition of the topic, read a core verse, look at an episode from Jesus' life that illustrates the topic, describe how this topic has been important in your life, or use a myriad of other ideas.
- **Motivation:** Why should the woman you're discipling be interested in this topic? In this part of your package, you address relevance. Share an illustration, a personal story, verses, or a biblical example to help her understand how the topic relates to her life as a follower of Christ.
- **Plan:** You want to do more than give someone information about a topic; you want to help her apply what she is learning. With this in mind, create a possible plan for how a woman

might make progress in this area. For example, ask yourself, *How can Elisa begin praying on a regular basis? Should she begin to keep a prayer list? What time of day and where might she pray?*

- **Examples/Illustrations:** Many disciplers I know keep a file of good illustrations and examples that relate to the topics they cover with other women. Once you begin developing packages of your own, your radar will be up as you read stories or hear sermon illustrations that apply to the key topics in your notebook.

- **Assignments/Resources:** Ask yourself, *What activity will help this woman further "own" the topic we're discussing?* Perhaps you can suggest a podcast or article on the topic that really helped you. Maybe there's a seminar coming up on the topic. One woman will respond to an invitation to journal about what she is learning. For another, interviewing another mature Christian woman about the topic increases her understanding and motivation. Don't overload a woman with assignments and resources; choose one that seems most suited to her personality. Or offer three possible assignments and let her select the one that motivates her the most.

- **Progress Check:** Decide how you will follow up with the woman you're helping. Perhaps you will call her every three days to ask how she's doing and if she has any questions. Keep these checkups light-handed. Your intention is not to instill guilt or browbeat. Rather, your goal is to find out what else—if anything—you might be able to do to help a woman take what she's been learning and make it a part of her life.

Now let's walk together through the process of creating a package. One of the first topics you'll probably want to address with the woman you disciple is the quiet time, which is a common term for daily, intentional time with God in the Word and prayer. Let's assume you are discipling a woman named Janet. Let's also assume that you've already done a topical Bible study on spending time with God and have selected key verses and passages.

1. Write your **objective** (for example, "To help Janet understand what a quiet time is and to show her how to have one").

2. Choose one of the following ideas for how you will **introduce** the topic (or add an idea of your own).

- Describe one of your recent quiet times and how you benefited from it (guidance, strength to resist temptation, encouragement, and so on).
- Read Mark 6. Talk about the pattern in Jesus' life of activity/ministry and retreat to pray and be with His Father. Point out that if Jesus needed time reserved for the Father, how much more do we.
- Other ideas:

3. Think through what might **motivate** Janet to make regular quiet times a part of her life. How is the practice of quiet time relevant to everyday life? Then complete this statement: "I am motivated to have daily quiet times because . . ." Your reasons might include the following: "God gives me guidance for everyday challenges," "I discover new insights into God's character, and that makes me love Him more," "I'm able to let go of my worries and fears when I'm in God's presence," and so on.

Do any of the verses you encountered in your topical study speak to the relevance or benefits of daily quiet times for everyday life? List those verses here.

4. Now it's time to help Janet with a **plan** for making regular quiet times a part of her life. One of the most effective ways to get a woman started with quiet times is to join her during them. It's always nice to do this face-to-face, maybe over a cup of coffee. But you can also have quiet times together over the phone. Here are some ways to get started:

- Select seven passages from the Gospels (one passage for each day) describing an event or encounter in Jesus' life. List them here.

- Select a few simple questions for Janet to ask herself about each passage. For instance, *What do I learn about Jesus from this passage? What do I learn about myself? What do I learn about living as a follower of Christ?*

- Give Janet the passages and questions. Set the logistics (for instance, "I'll call you every morning at eight after the kids have left for school. We can read the passage together over the phone, talk through the questions, and then pray together. Which days this week will work best for you?").

- Think about what roadblocks to quiet times Janet will likely encounter. What are some ways you can help her get past those roadblocks? What has worked for you?

5. If you are new at discipling, you may not yet have a hefty file of good **examples and illustrations** that relate to quiet time. Your pastor, Bible study leader, and other mature Christians you know may be good resources at this point in your preparation. Ask them if they know of any stories from the lives of famous Christians that illustrate the value of quiet times in a believer's life. Or invite them to describe the benefits of quiet time that they've personally experienced. Tape them (audio or video) as they tell their stories (it's always effective to vary the ways in which you deliver content to the women you disciple).

6. Next you want to think through any additional **assignments and resources** that might help Janet with quiet times. What tools, methods, books, and articles have helped you stay faithful to daily times with the Lord? Select one or two to suggest to Janet.

7. Keep track of Janet's **progress**. After the two of you have completed seven quiet times together, talk with her about how she'll continue this practice on her own. Help her identify a time, place, and length of time for her daily encounters with the Lord. When you meet for your regular one-to-one times, always ask Janet what discoveries she has made during the previous week's quiet times. If she is struggling with making quiet times a habit, talk together about possible solutions.

Write here other ideas for following up with Janet.

LET'S EVALUATE

Now you can rejoice! You have created your first customized package for a woman you're discipling. The steps you just walked through can be adapted to every topic you want to cover. So how was this process? On a scale of 1 (easy as pie) to 10 (nearly did me in), how would you rate your experience in writing a package on quiet time?

Remember what I mentioned earlier: Some will thrive on this exercise, some will find it helpful for a season, and others will be so grounded in the basics of the faith that they can wing it as they meet with other women.

Your attitude toward preparing these packages may be influenced by one last perspective: The benefits of preparing discipling packages aren't for you alone, the discipler. As you walk through each topic with the women you disciple, your model will encourage them to begin creating their own packages (or adapting and personalizing yours) to use with the women they will one day disciple. Much of the value of these packages is their pass-along nature. Over the years, dozens of women could end up benefiting from some version of a single package that you prepared.

TIPS AS YOU PREPARE TO MEET ONE TO ONE

Let's assume that you have someone to disciple, you have packages for the first few topics you plan to cover with her, and you are about to start meeting. We've already talked in previous chapters about meeting logistics, such as where, when, and how long. But now let's look at the essential area of preparing yourself.

- **Be prayerful.** Before you meet, ask God to help you set aside all the other "stuff" of your day and focus on Him and the woman you are about to meet with.
- **Be warm.** Enjoy some small talk. Share what you've been up to. Talk about your kids, hobbies, work, and so on. Don't treat your meetings as business transactions ("You show up; I impart information") but instead enjoy the blossoming relationship.

- **Be relaxed.** No matter how well you prepare, you will fumble for words or lose your train of thought or get your papers mixed up. Laugh at yourself and move on. Women will be delighted to see that you are human just like them.
- **Be real.** I love these words from Jill Briscoe, "After all we are not expected to be models of perfection, but models of growth and learning."[1]

You don't want to come across as the all-wise one, seated upon a pedestal. Instead come alongside the women you disciple as a fellow pilgrim—as their companion on the journey of drawing closer to Christ, not as someone who has already "arrived." Heather Hanneman, age 33, of Boulder, Colorado, reminds us, "Share what God is teaching you at this season of your life and live your life authentically, both the joys and struggles."

- **Keep an open grasp as you engage with women!** Any woman you have the privilege of helping does not belong to you! She belongs to God. Not every relationship will last long. Some will not flourish. And, some might even end up feeling hurtful! Cathy Bowman, age 59, from State College, Pennsylvania, points out, "Sometimes the person realizes she doesn't really want help. At other times, we may discover we want to get together as peers or friends but not in a structured setting. And sometimes the timing just isn't right for what God is doing in their lives or mine."
- **Be Jesus-centered.** When Jesus commanded us to make disciples in Matthew 28:18-20, the word He used was *matheteuo*. *Matheteuo* means not only to learn from but also to become attached to one's teacher and become his follower in doctrine and conduct of life. What we always need to keep in mind is that we want women to become attached to Jesus, not to us. So

---

1. Jill Briscoe, *Here Am I, Lord . . . Send Somebody Else* (Nashville, TN: W Publishing Group, 2004), 44.

whatever tools and plans and procedures we use as we disciple another woman, we must ask above all, *Am I helping this woman become attached to Christ? Am I helping her to learn dependence on her Savior?* In her book *If,* Amy Carmichael says it so clearly: "If I slip into the place that can be filled by Christ alone, making myself the first necessity to a soul instead of leading it to fasten upon Him, then I know nothing of Calvary love."[2]

WORDS OF ENCOURAGEMENT

We've covered a lot in this chapter! Let's close with comments from Meaghan (who was discipled) and Lori (who discipled her). I find in their words such motivation to keep on investing my life in helping other women walk more intimately with their Lord. I hope you do too.

From my times with Lori, in which we studied the Bible and prayed together, I discovered lies I believed about myself and hidden sin that was holding me back from experiencing the freedom Christ intended for me. Having someone speak into my life who knew me on such a deep level really helped me grow. Such growth would have taken a lot longer without Lori.

— MEAGHAN HART, AGE 23, COLORADO SPRINGS, COLORADO

Meeting with Meaghan was more of a blessing than I could have imagined. I loved my times with her, and God used her to teach and challenge me. She has become a dear friend and a kindred spirit. We both experienced engagement and marriage at around the same time. Walking through life with her has been a delight. When I see and hear how she and her husband are living for the Lord, I am filled with incredible joy!

— LORI BUTLER, AGE 28, TUCSON, ARIZONA

2. Amy Carmichael, *If* (Fort Washington, PA: Christian Literature Crusade), 66.

Sample Package

Topic: *His Word Is Your Life!*
Deuteronomy 32:47

Objective:

To help her embrace the Word of God as vital and necessary for her life.

Introduction:

In a dry tone share this silly story: When I first dated my husband, Tom, we never spoke to one another. It was great. For years he never said a word to me. Obviously this did not happen. Do you think that it is possible to have a relationship if you never hear a word from the one you are drawn to? Not possible.

God has spoken to us through His Word. As we take in His Word we get to know Him better and our relationship grows.

Motivation:

Ask: How do people today generally view the Bible or the Scriptures?

How do you view the Word of God?

Examples:

- If you bought a car would you want the owner's manual? Why?
- If you were going to make a dress what would you need beside fabric? Pattern with instructions?
- If you were driving to a new location what would be essential to take with you? A map of where you were going?
- Read 1 Peter 2:2. How is the Word for the believer like milk for a baby?

God has not left us alone as we journey in knowing Him. He has given us His Word!

Continued on the next page

Continued from the previous page

Plan:

Today we will look at and discuss five essential characteristics of the Word.

There are more characteristics but these are absolutely vital!

1. The Word of God is **Inspired**
   2 Timothy 3:16
   2 Peter 1:20-21
   Why is it important to know that the Word of God is inspired? What difference does it make?

2. The Word of God is **True**
   John 17:17
   Numbers 23:19
   How does knowing that God's Word is Truth stimulate you to know the Word?

3. The Word of God is **Living**
   John 6:63
   Hebrews 4:12
   What picture comes to mind when you see how the living Word is described in Hebrews 4:12?

4. The Word of God is **Vital**
   Matthew 4:4
   Jeremiah 15:16
   If Jesus memorized the Word and used it as a tool as He opposed Satan what does that say for us?

5. The Word of God is **Powerful**
   Jeremiah 23:29
   Ephesians 6:17
   The sword is an offensive weapon. Compare the Word to a powerful sword.

Continued on the next page

Continued from the previous page

Discuss these characteristics using the questions to stimulate discussion. End the overall discussion with this question: Which of these characteristics do you find most amazing . . . hard to believe . . . super . . . important . . . etc.? How do these characteristics motivate you as you spend time alone with God each day in His Word?

Assignment:

Knowing these characteristics motivate us to deepen our intake of the Word of God. Discuss how it is going for her as she spends time in God's Word on a daily basis. Talk about what she would like to do to strengthen this habit. Ask how I might give her accountability in this.

Possibly assign one of the following resources:

- Resource: Invite her to go to www.discipleshiplibrary.com and listen to the 3 ½ minute tape by Leroy Eims titled, *The Word: 2 Timothy 3:16*
- Resource: Read Chapter 5 of *More Than a Carpenter* by Josh McDowell
- Resource: The Hand Illustration: Ask if she has seen this illustration and if not plan on sharing The Hand next time.

Close:

Read Joshua 1:8. Ask: What did God say to Joshua about His book as He stepped up as the next leader of Israel? In light of the characteristics of His Word that we studied today why do you think God said this to Joshua?

Pray together or pray for her:

Pray and thank God for each of these five characteristics. Ask Him to confirm one of these essential characteristics of His Word in her life this week as she spends time with Him in His Word. Ask also for His blessing and a deeper awareness of Him as she spends daily time in His Word.

CHAPTER 10

Discipling Like Jesus

Jesus said to them, "Follow Me,
and I will make you become fishers of men."
(MARK 1:17, NASB)

As You sent Me into the world,
I also have sent them into the world.
(JOHN 17:18, NASB)

MOST OF THE women I know are great at building relationships. It seems to be second nature for women to create opportunities to spend time together. Therefore, the relational connection so vital in discipling comes fairly naturally to us.

But there is also an intentional side of discipling that can create havoc for many women. Too often, if we are purposeful and focused in a relationship—if we have a goal (even a good one)—we grow uncomfortable. We rightly cringe at the potential of turning a relationship into a project. Yet who of us has looked at Jesus with His disciples and even considered for a moment that they were mere projects to Him? Jesus is the ultimate Discipler, perfectly relational and perfectly intentional, and we can benefit from observing Him in the Gospels.

OBSERVING THE MASTER DISCIPLER

1. Read Mark 1:17 and 2:14. Jesus not only invited these men to *do* something, He invited them to *become* something! What did He invite them to do?

2. What did He invite them to become? How does this show intentionality on His part?

3. What does Mark 1:38 reveal about why Jesus came to earth?

4. According to Mark 3:13-14, what did Jesus recruit the Twelve to do?

5. What do you think is meant by "be with him"? What is the significance of this phrase when you consider the relational ability and intentionality of Jesus?

6. How does this "with him/her" principle affect how you view your discipling relationships?

7. Jesus selected twelve men to be with Him. Yet in Mark 13:3 and 14:33, we see a different pattern of discipling. What is happening in these verses?

8. What additional aspect of the "with him/her" principle does this suggest?

The passages we've looked at so far give us a glimpse into how Jesus related to those He chose to disciple. Now let's look at what He modeled for His disciples.

9. Read Mark 1:35-38 and Luke 6:12-13. What did Jesus model for His men here?

10. What immediately followed these two occasions when Jesus prayed in solitude? What does that tell you about the value of prayer for you as a discipler?

11. What does one of Jesus' disciples ask for in Luke 11:1?

12. How does that request reflect the effectiveness of Jesus' intentionality in modeling a prayerful life?

We can define and dissect discipling in a lot of ways, but it is really quite simple. It is about being relational and intentional with those whom God entrusts to us. As we examine the life of Christ, especially in the book of Mark, we see three ways Jesus intentionally imparted His life.

- He taught them.
- He prayed for them.
- He modeled what He wanted them to become.

I am challenged when I see the way Jesus lived so intentionally. He gave His life to His disciples "that they might be with Him" and so He could impart His vision and life to them fully. He had a clear mission and nothing distracted Him — not the tyranny of the urgent, not weariness, not persecution. He was single-minded and committed to giving His life to what the Father had sent Him to do. I am challenged to live this passionate, single-minded life of Christ!
— Jennifer Johnson, age 33, Manhattan, Kansas

My favorite definition of discipleship is borrowed from Evan Griffin, Navigator Staff: friendship with a vision. It's the art of taking a woman where she is presently, seeing who she could become if she embraced the truth of Scripture (vision), and taking steps to bring her there in relationship with you and Jesus.
— Kim Havenstein, age 37, Lincoln, Nebraska

INSIGHTS FROM A DISCIPLER'S PRAYER

In John 17, we get to listen to Jesus pray. This is the prayer that Jesus offered up as He was about to be betrayed by Judas and arrested by Roman officers. From this prayer, we can reap rich insight into Jesus' intentions for living among and training the twelve disciples.

13. Read John 17:1-21. According to verses 6 and 9, where did Jesus' disciples come from?

14. How does this affect the way you think of the women you are discipling?

15. How does Jesus describe what He did while He was with these disciples (see verses 7-8)?

16. How does this correspond with what you've been learning about preparing topics and content for those you disciple?

17. What do verses 11-15 tell you about what to pray for those you disciple?

18. Read verse 17. What does *sanctify* mean? If you aren't sure, use a Bible dictionary, study Bible, or online Bible resource to research an answer.

19. According to this verse, how does sanctification take place?

20. As Jesus prays to His Father He requests, "Sanctify them by the truth, your *Word* is truth." What does this request tell you about the importance of helping those you disciple get into God's Word and apply its truths to their lives?

John 17 impresses me with two things: One is that *God* gives us women to disciple. We don't manufacture discipling opportunities. God entrusts us with the lives of women to invest in. Second, the purpose of our investment in another woman's life is her sanctification through His Word. Jesus says in John 17:17, "Sanctify them by the truth; your Word is truth." If I want to help another woman grow, I need to prioritize the Word in our times together in such a way that she receives His Word as authoritative and worthy of her obedience.

21. In verse 20, Jesus expands His prayer. What does this verse imply about Jesus' expectation for the men He has helped?

Scott Morton, in his book *Down-to-Earth Discipling*, says this about John 17:

> In verse 20 . . . [Jesus] fully expects His disciples to be fruitful in bringing the gospel to others. His goal is bigger than mentoring the twelve. Reaching the third generation was in His mind from the beginning.[1]

Here's how this idea of generations captured the heart of one discipler:

> *Generations to me means seeing my life multiplied spiritually into the lives of women who will in turn passionately walk with Christ and devote their lives to seeing the next generation reached with the gospel. My biggest desire is to live for something that will outlast me, and I am trusting God that there will be women all over the world who are pursuing Christ and laboring for Him as a result of God's using my life and the lives of the women I've invested in. There is so little I can do by myself, but by giving my life to others who can in turn give their lives to others, the potential impact is limitless! I am convinced that there is just no other way the world will be reached for Christ. I cling to John 12:24 when I think about spiritual discipling: "I tell you the truth, unless a kernel of wheat falls to the ground and dies, it remains only a single seed. But if it dies, it produces many seeds."*
> — JENNIFER JOHNSON, AGE 33, MANHATTAN, KANSAS

22. We've been looking at Jesus' example as a discipler who was both relational and intentional. Read the John 17 prayer one more time. How is the relational side of Jesus' discipling revealed in this prayer?

---

1. Scott Morton, *Down-to-Earth Discipling: Essential Principles to Guide Your Personal Ministry* (Colorado Springs, CO: NavPress, 2003), 110.

23. How is His intentional side revealed?

24. Identify what you feel are the two or three most significant things you've learned from this study about how Jesus discipled others. List them here and then write out how you want these observations from Jesus' life to influence how you disciple other women.

IF YOU CAN'T GET ENOUGH

Over the coming months, you might want to read the book of Mark, focusing on these things:

- What topics did Jesus teach to His disciples?
- What did Jesus model for His disciples?
- What did Jesus pray for His disciples?
- How are both the relational and intentional sides of Jesus' discipling revealed in this gospel?

Words in Closing

PRESENTLY I AM fifty-eight years old. . . . the training and material development I have entrusted to you in this workbook was entrusted to me when I was in my twenties. At this time, though I am involved in many ministry activities, I meet regularly with two young women. Both have sensitive hearts to God's Spirit. Both want to grow. Both are still taking in all that it means to belong to Jesus. They are becoming like Christ and seeking to contribute and build in the lives of others.

The older I get the more I realize the essential value of helping others know Christ through His Word and prayer. If I were to pick only two topics to strengthen someone in it would be these. By taking root in His Word all the person of Christ and all there is to know of discipleship would be available to them. By learning to pray, in essence, they learn to open their heart to Jesus. The Word, God speaking to us, and prayer, us speaking with Him, creates the basic foundation for conversation with God for a lifetime; an eternal life time!

"This is eternal life: that they may know you, the only true God, and Jesus Christ, whom you have sent." (John 17:3)

About the Author

DANA AND HER HUSBAND, TOM, have been on staff with the Navigators since 1978. They served at Purdue University working with graduate student couples before moving overseas in 1984 as missionaries to Indonesia. Upon returning in 1994 they accepted the opportunity to help direct the U.S. Collegiate Navigators. Dana served as an Associate Director of the U.S. Collegiate Ministry overseeing the needs of women staff from 1995-2002.

From 2002-2006 Dana worked with Learning Rx, a business company, as a Trainer, Account Executive, and local Center Director.

Dana and Tom have three adult children and five grandchildren. Besides playing with grandkids, Dana speaks to women's groups, meets one-to-one with women, and also serves with her husband, Tom, as he coaches leaders in several European countries. She also facilitates a monthly gathering of women at Glen Eyrie called "Flourish."

As a mentor it is her passion to see women, both young and old, grow spiritually as they walk closer with Jesus through His Word and prayer.